Contents

Getting a fair deal

Whenever you buy goods or pay for a service, you enter into a 'contract' with the seller. This contract gives both of you certain rights and obligations, which today are well defined in law. However, you don't have to rely solely on the law for protection. Codes of Practice, for instance, adopted by many trade associations for their members to follow, give you benefits over and above your legal rights. Various bodies watch over your interests as a consumer, and in several cases deal with complaints. Labelling schemes tell you facts you need to know before you buy, or assure you that a product is safe in normal use. And finally there are many things you can do to help yourself.

There is no better way of getting a fair deal than by understanding your rights and obligations, and by buying wisely. To help in this there are consumer columns in newspapers and magazines, and programmes on radio and TV. You could also join a national or local consumer group (or help to start one if there isn't one in your area).

This booklet, therefore, isn't just about your legal rights. It tells you about the other measures designed to protect, how to complain if things go wrong, and where to turn for advice and help.

The law of the land

Before you read about your rights as a consumer, it is a good idea to learn a little about the nature of the law in this country.

Criminal law discourages behaviour which can be harmful to the community as a whole – theft and drunken driving for example – and, in the field of consumer protection, deliberate fraud, sharp practice and dangerous acts such as selling bad food or electrically unsafe appliances. Offenders are prosecuted, either by Trading Standards and Environmental Health Officers or by the police. In Scotland prosecutions are almost always brought by procurators fiscal. Punishments can be fines, imprisonment or both. In England, Wales and Scotland the courts can order compensation for personal injury, loss or damage to those who have suffered as a result of someone's criminal activity. Redress for the purchaser of faulty goods, however, is mainly a matter for the civil law.

Civil law governs the rights and obligations that individuals have towards other individuals. For example, when you buy goods from a shop, the sale is governed by the civil law of contract. If the goods are faulty and the trader refuses to put the matter right, it is open to you, the buyer, to enforce your rights under civil law by suing in the courts.

Statutory law: Both criminal and civil law can be statutory, that is, contained in acts of Parliament. For example, the Trade Descriptions Acts (see page 20) are *criminal*, while the Sale of Goods Act (see page 5) is *civil*.

Many acts passed today give the Government powers to make rules when these are needed. Such rules are generally either 'orders' or 'regulations' (some are mentioned in this booklet).

Common law is law which is not contained in statutes, but has developed over the years from, among other things, decisions made by judges in court cases. For example, the obligation on a trader to carry out any contract for the provision of services 'in a proper and workmanlike manner' comes not from statute but from common law.

There are some differences between the laws of England and Wales and those of Scotland and Northern Ireland and these are noted in this booklet in the appropriate places.

Your rights when buying goods

Buying from traders

Millions of shopping transactions are made each year, most of them quite satisfactorily. But occasionally something goes wrong and it's worthwhile knowing what rights you have if you need to complain.

Here are three typical shopping problems

1 You've just bought a pair of shoes. After a week, the seams come apart and the heel on one shoe wobbles. You haven't treated them badly nor used them in circumstances for which they were not intended. **Can you insist on a pair to replace them?**

2 You want an electric food mixer. You choose one and ask the manager if it is powerful enough to knead bread dough. He assures you it is. But when you use it on your bread, the mixer can't cope. The shop doesn't have another model of any use to you and offers a credit note. You, however, want a refund so you can buy elsewhere. **Have you the right to demand one?**

3 You send for a blue blanket from a mail order company. It turns out to be pink even though the box is labelled 'blue'. You don't want the pink one (it doesn't match your colour scheme) nor do you want to pay for the return postage. **Can you claim for the postage at the same time as you ask for the correct blanket?**

What are your rights in situations like these?

Sale of Goods Act 1979

The answers are in the *Sale of Goods Act 1979* which covers all goods (including food) bought from a trader, whether from shops, street markets, doorstep salesmen, in sales, at parties in private homes, or by mail order. It doesn't make any difference whether the goods are paid for in cash or by credit. Once the seller has accepted your offer to buy, he takes on obligations which are part of his contract. (It doesn't matter if neither of you has spoken or written anything about the goods; your offer to buy and his acceptance count as a contract.)

The seller has three main obligations:

1 that the goods are of 'merchantable quality'

'Merchantable quality' means that goods must be reasonably fit for their normal purpose, bearing in mind the price paid, the nature of the goods and how they were described.

The new shoes in example **1** shouldn't fall apart after only a week's normal wear; and the wheels of your new shopping trolley shouldn't come off on its first outing. If goods are very cheap, secondhand, bought in as 'seconds', or 'sale' items, you probably cannot expect top quality – but they must still be merchantable.

2 that the goods are 'fit for any particular purpose' made known to him

If you ask for goods, like the food mixer in example **2**, to perform in a particular way, and the seller assures you that they will, he has broken his contract with you if they do not.

3 that the goods are 'as described'

Goods must be 'as described' – for example on the package, display sign or by the seller. The blanket in example **3** did not meet the description applied to it.

Getting money back

If any of these obligations have not been met the seller has broken his contract with you and you may be entitled to money back or compensation.

*You should always complain to the seller, **not** to the manufacturer, since in law it is the seller who is responsible for the goods (but see page 11 for manufacturer's liability).*

Legally, traders should collect faulty goods. But unless the article is large, heavy or liable to damage if moved incorrectly, it is usually best to take it back yourself. That way you can discuss the problem face to face, and it is much quicker. Remember, it will help both you and the trader if you explain the problem in a calm and courteous way.

You may be able to get all your money back **or** a cash payment to make up the difference between what you paid for the goods and their reduced value. Exactly what you are entitled to depends on how serious the fault is, how much use you got out of the goods and how soon you tell the seller about the problem.

You have the right to include in your claim any additional expenses such as travel or return postage (see example **3,** on page 5). If you have to hire similar goods while yours are out of action, you may be able to get compensation for this too.

You may be able to claim extra compensation if you suffer loss or personal injury because of faulty goods – for example, when a brand new iron when correctly used ruins clothes or gives you a nasty shock. Even if you accepted a free repair to your iron you could still claim compensation for your damaged clothes.

You are not entitled to anything if you:
- examined the item when you bought it and the faults were so obvious that you should have seen them.

- were told about any specific fault (for example, the goods were described as 'fire damaged').

- ignored the seller's skill or judgment as to the suitability of goods for any particular purpose you described to him (for example, he told you the food mixer you were buying wouldn't knead bread dough – as you wished).

- ignored the seller's claim that he wasn't expert enough to advise you correctly about your purchase (for example, he told you he didn't know whether the glue you were buying would stick metal to plastic).

- simply changed you mind about wanting the article. Some shops do refund money or give credit notes, but they do so for commercial goodwill and not because they have to. However, traders will not usually take back something you've damaged or bought from another shop.

- got it as a present (the **buyer** must make any claim).

Replacements or repairs

You could, if you wished, accept a replacement or a repair, but the trader is not obliged to offer anything except cash compensation.

Credit notes

You do not have to accept a credit note for faulty goods. If you do, you may have difficulty getting your money back later when you find nothing else you like. Remember too that credit notes are sometimes valid for only a limited period.

'No refunds' notices

Don't be put off by notices saying 'No money refunded', even for sale goods. Such notices are illegal and should be reported to the local Trading Standards Officer (see page 54). As explained on page 26, a trader cannot wriggle out of his responsibility if he sells you **faulty** goods.

Secondhand goods

When a trader sells something secondhand it will probably not be in perfect condition, but it is still covered by the Sale of Goods Act. An upholstered chair may have a few snags in the covering but it should be of merchantable quality and fit for its purpose – that is, capable of being sat upon safely – unless of course, it is sold as being in need of structural repair.

Your right to compensation will depend on many factors, including the price paid, the age of the article, and how it was described.

For example, if you bought a reconditioned vacuum cleaner said to be only three years old and in excellent condition, but it didn't work when you got it home, you might be able to get a full refund or the cost of the repairs needed.

As with new goods, you can't complain about defects that were pointed out to you or which you should have seen if you examined them.

It is a good idea to take someone with you to note what is said about an expensive secondhand item. In the case of cars, it's best to arrange an independent technical inspection before you agree to buy.

See page 13 for your rights when buying goods privately.

Sales

Many people don't realise that sale items are covered by all the rules in the Sale of Goods Act. Goods bought in a sale must, for example, be of merchantable quality and perform the tasks for which they were made. Two examples:

1 You buy an electric kettle, reduced in price because of a dent in its lid. When you get it home it doesn't work because of an electrical fault. You are entitled to compensation (see page 7) because the kettle doesn't boil water as it is supposed to do, and you couldn't reasonably be expected to know about the electrical fault.

2 By contrast, if you buy a glass water jug described as a 'second' and later find a slight flaw in its decoration, you are not entitled to any compensation. You should have known it would have some defect and it is still of merchantable quality, bearing in mind its description and, probably, low price.

The law also covers the display of prices for sale goods, and certain 'bargain offer' claims (see page 17).

Trading stamps, tokens and coupons

Goods given in exchange for stamps, tokens or coupons must be of merchantable quality. If not, you are entitled to compensation. If the supplier agrees, you may prefer to accept a replacement or something of the same face value instead.

Can your rights be taken away?

The Unfair Contract Terms Act (page 26) prohibits a trader from 'contracting out' of his obligations under the Sale of Goods Act. Additionally, an order made under the Fair Trading Act 1973 prohibits the use of any statement in, for example, a contract, order form, invoice, or guarantee, which seems to take away your rights. The trader concerned could be prosecuted. If you receive a document containing such a statement, either strike it out or ignore it. You should, however, draw it to the attention of the shop – it could be on old stationery, and a genuine mistake. But tell the local Trading Standards Officer if you suspect a deliberate attempt to deny you your rights. The Unfair Contract Terms Act also protects you from a trader trying to avoid responsibility for death or injury arising from his negligence.

Manufacturer's liability

Under the Sale of Goods Act the retailer who sold the goods is responsible for compensating the buyer if they are faulty. But quite apart from compensation for the goods them-selves, there are occasions when you may be able to sue the manufacturer. These are when you have been injured or your property damaged *and* when it can be proved that the injury or damage arose out of the manufacturer's negligence. ('You' in this context can mean anyone, not just the actual buyer.) It doesn't matter whether or not you've signed the manu-facturer's guarantee – the manufacturer is liable for unsafe goods and a guarantee cannot take away this liability.

Goods on order

Suppose you want something for a particular occasion (for example, a bridesmaid's dress) and the shop has to obtain the goods specially for you. You will probably want to give a date by which they must be supplied. Provided the shop agrees to your conditions (which are best put in writing), it is legally bound to have the goods ready for you by that date. If it fails to do so, it has broken its contract with you. You have the right to cancel your order and ask for your money back. You may also sue for compensation if you were forced to spend more money as a result of the non-supply of the goods (for example, if you had to hire a bridesmaid's dress at the last moment).

Even if you don't agree a date with the trader, he still has to supply the goods within a 'reasonable' time. What is reason-able for certain kinds of goods may not be reasonable for

others. A plastic pedal bin 'ex stock' might arrive within a few days but a settee upholstered in a fabric of your own choice might take many weeks. If you think a reasonable time has passed and you don't want to wait forever, contact the shop and agree a **final** date for supply. State clearly (preferably in writing) that if the goods haven't come by that date you will cancel them and want your money back. If, however, you do agree to wait the longer time, you cannot cancel in that period without breaking your side of the bargain. The shop could be entitled to keep any deposit paid and even sue you for more money.

A mail order trader must also send you goods in a reasonable time. If he makes his own deliveries you can agree a date by when you want the goods. If they don't arrive on time you can refuse to accept them. But a mail order firm often uses a carrier (the Post Office, British Rail, or a van service). In this case the firm must make reasonable arrangements on your behalf – that is, choose an appropriate means of carriage, pack the goods properly and deliver them to the carrier in a reasonable time. If there is a long delay, and you have evidence that the goods were actually sent by the mail order firm to the carrier, all you can do is complain to the carrier. (See also page 61 for the extra protection which Codes of Practice give when buying by mail order.)

Buying privately

When you buy something privately, only one of the obligations of the Sale of Goods Act applies: the item must be **as described** (see page 6).

Your other rights will depend on what is said between you and the seller – that is, what you were told about its value and condition. If the goods are faulty, your remedy will probably be to sue for misrepresentation, since protection under the Sale of Goods Act regarding **merchantable quality** and **fitness for any particular purpose** applies only to people who are selling as traders.

It is a good idea to take along a friend who is knowledgeable about the particular item, or who could act as witness, when you buy something expensive from a private seller.

Some traders, operating from their homes, use the 'small ads' columns in newspapers to sell their goods. This is fine as long as they make it clear that they **are** traders!

But some pose as private sellers – a practice that is illegal – because they can make you think you have fewer rights, that is, those relating to **merchantable quality** and **fitness for any particular purpose**.

If you buy something faulty through a 'small ad', and you suspect the seller is a trader 'in disguise', tell your local Trading Standards Officer. If the seller in fact turns out to be a trader you can seek redress under the Sale of Goods Act.

Auctions

Whereas in all other contracts with consumers for the sale of goods, traders cannot get out of their responsibility for seeing that goods are of merchantable quality, as described and fit for any purpose demanded by the buyer, auctioneers can legally do so. However, you may challenge an auctioneer in court if it seems unreasonable for him to rely on any statement denying his responsibility.

If you go to an auction, read any notices and catalogues carefully. They may give conditions of sale about such things as payment, deposits and removal of the goods. Look at the goods before the sale to see if they are really what you want and of good enough quality for the maximum price you intend to pay. Remember, the moment the auctioneer's hammer falls, he accepts the last bid – and it could be yours!

More things you should know when buying goods

Shops don't have to sell

A trader doesn't have to sell an article. For instance, he may not wish to disturb a window display; or he may have made a mistake by pricing goods too low and be unwilling to lose the profit by selling at that price. It is up to the trader to either accept or refuse your offer to buy.

Receipts

A trader doesn't have to give a receipt or check-out slip, but there is no harm in asking for one. If a receipt is given, keep it for a while as it is an excellent proof of purchase if you have to complain about faulty goods. But do not be put off by signs such as 'No refunds without receipts', which imply that complaints won't be dealt with unless you produce a receipt. Such signs have no effect on your legal rights, and are in fact prohibited (see page 8).

Price display

With few exceptions (see page 19), a trader doesn't have to display prices for his goods.

Unless anything is said to the contrary, it is assumed that when you contract to buy goods you are agreeing to buy them at the currently displayed price including Value Added Tax (VAT) if applicable. Apart from prices for food and drink consumed on the premises, which must by law be VAT-inclusive and displayed at the point where consumers can make their choice, traders may, if they wish, display a notice saying 'All prices are exclusive of VAT'.

As explained earlier, a trader doesn't have to sell you goods, but he commits an offence under the Trade Descriptions Act 1968 (see page 20) if he deliberately displays a price on something which is less than the price he actually charges for it.

Price increases and reductions

With goods on order, the price you pay will depend on what you and the seller agree. If he is getting in new stock specially to meet your demand he may ask you to pay the manufacturer's increased price at the time of delivery. If he doesn't say (or write) anything about a price increase, you should have to pay only the price you saw when you placed your order. Either way, make sure you know where you stand, preferably by getting the details in writing.

When you order from a catalogue or brochure which says something like 'subject to price fluctuations' or 'prices correct at time of going to print' you are bound to pay the current price.

You will have to pay any increase in VAT unless the trader decides to absorb it in his profit or unless the contract specifically says no alterations in VAT will be passed on.

There is a ban on the repricing of food items which are on the shelves and marked with a price, unless the alteration relates to VAT (although very few food items carry VAT). There is also an exception for 'special' or 'introductory offer' prices on food.

'Special offers', 'fantastic bargains', 'prices slashed' – these are only a few of the slogans traders use to entice you into their shops, particularly for the winter and summer sales. But are the goods they offer really such bargains? Under the Trade Descriptions Act 1968 (see page 20), some kinds of 'double pricing' or false price reductions are banned. A shopkeeper must not offer goods for sale at a marked-down price unless **either** they were on offer at the old price for at least 28 consecutive days in the last six months **or** he states clearly that this is not the case. It is also an offence to suggest in any way that the price of any item is less than it really is.

'Bargain offer' claims

By an order made under the Prices Act 1974 (see page 19), certain misleading or uninformative 'bargain offer' claims about a trader's prices for goods or services are prohibited if compared with another price. For example, expressions like 'worth £x – our price £y', 'saving up to 50% on prices elsewhere' must not be used. Comparisons with insurance valuations are also illegal. You can tell the local Trading Standards Officer (see page 54) about any notices or advertisements which you think might be breaking the law.

'Recommended' retail prices

Also under the Prices Act, comparisons with manufacturers' 'recommended' retail prices are illegal for some products. To date these are beds, carpets, furniture, domestic electrical (and other powered) appliances and consumer electronic products.

Consumer Safety Acts

The Consumer Safety Act 1978 widens the scope of the Consumer Protection Acts 1961 and 1971 (and the 1965 legislation for Northern Ireland), which it will eventually repeal. It enables the Secretary of State for Trade to require that goods be labelled with, for example, warning symbols, instructions for use, or lists of ingredients. It also enables the Secretary of State to take rapid action to ban the sale of dangerous goods and requires the supplier to issue warnings about goods already sold. For example, regulations have been made banning the sale of ornamental glitter lamps and Tris-treated textile articles (both of which contain dangerous chemicals) and – unless it carries a label warning of the dangers – new upholstered furniture not resistant to cigarettes and matches (see page 46).

The earlier Acts gave the Secretary of State power to make regulations in respect of any type of goods to prevent or reduce the risk of death or personal injury. There are regulations relating to the safety of domestic electrical heating appliances, carry-cot stands, cooking utensils, pencils and crayons, children's nightdresses and domestic oil lamps. (Equivalent regulations exist under the Northern Ireland Act of 1965.)

Under both new and old Acts it is a criminal offence to sell goods which do not comply with the regulations. This applies where the goods are sold in the course of business and covers, in most cases, second-hand goods as well as new.

Food and Drugs Acts

The Food and Drugs Act 1955 makes it a criminal offence to sell unfit food, or to describe food falsely, or to mislead people about its nature, substance, or quality, including the nutritional value. Regulations cover food hygiene wherever food is sold, manufactured, packed, processed or stored for sale; food labelling (name of the contents, list of ingredients, and address of labeller or packer for use in complaints); and food composition (such as how much meat is in a sausage), control of food additives and contaminants. Local authorities (in Northern Ireland, District Councils) are responsible for enforcing these regulations. Scotland is covered by the Food and Drugs (Scotland) Act 1956 and Northern Ireland by the Food and Drugs Act (Northern Ireland) 1958.

Under the Food and Drugs (Control of Food Premises) Act 1976, when someone has been convicted under the food hygiene regulations, the courts can close down his premises if they find that they are insanitary and a danger to health. (There are equivalent provisions for Scotland and Northern Ireland.)

Prices Act 1974

This Act enables the Government to require prices to be displayed and to control the way in which they are displayed. Shops must mark prices for all items of food and drink except where sold by counter service.

For certain foods which are commonly sold by weight – such as meat and most (though not all) fruit and vegetables – unit prices (for example, price per lb) must be indicated. Pubs, cafes and restaurants must display a selection of prices for meals and drinks. Garages have to display the price of petrol on the pump.

Certain 'bargain offer' claims are prohibited and comparisons with 'recommended' prices are also banned in particular sectors (see page 17). There is also a ban on increasing the price of food items which have been on sale and marked with a price (page 16).

Local Trading Standards Officers enforce these parts of the Prices Act.

Trade Descriptions Acts 1968 and 1972

The Trade Descriptions Act 1968 makes it a criminal offence for a trader to describe his goods falsely, whether in written or spoken form, or by illustration. This applies to many different kinds of description – what the goods are, who made them, how they work, and so on. If a car has 20,000 miles on the clock or a trader tells you 'This pan has a non-stick coating', these statements must be true. Similarly, if a photograph on the label of a packet of prawn curry shows lots of juicy prawns, the contents must live up to the description. In the case of textile products, special regulations ensure that the fibre content is marked on them. Under this Act some kinds of false price reductions or 'markdowns' are illegal, and traders must not suggest that the price of goods is less than it really is (page 17). The Trade Descriptions Act 1968 also affects services (see page 25).

Under the two Acts there are certain obligations on retailers to indicate the country of origin of goods. By an order made under the 1968 Act, textiles, floor coverings, clothing, footwear, metal cutlery and domestic electrical appliances must be marked or accompanied by a clear indication of such origin. Under the 1972 Act, any new goods carrying the name of a UK business or place-name of somewhere in the UK must, if they were manufactured outside the UK, carry a clear indication of their real country of manufacture.

The local Trading Standards Officer enforces the Trade Descriptions Acts, which also give him power to enter premises, inspect and seize goods. If you suspect the law is being broken you should let him know. He may decide to prosecute. If convicted, a trader can be fined or imprisoned. In England, Wales and Scotland the courts can award you compensation if you have suffered as a result of the offence. You may, of course, sue the trader yourself.

Unsolicited Goods and Services Act 1971

Under this Act, a trader can be fined if he demands payment for goods he knows you haven't ordered. If you receive an invoice for goods you never ordered, take it to the local Trading Standards Officer.

If you are sent goods you didn't ask for by a trader who is hoping to make a sale, and you don't want to buy them, they nevertheless become your property if he doesn't take them back within six months of your receiving them. You can then use them, sell them or otherwise dispose of them as if they had been a gift. You can, if you prefer, cut short the six months' period by writing to the sender, giving your name and address, and stating that the goods were 'unsolicited'. If he fails to collect them within 30 days, they become yours to do with as you like. But in either case you must give the sender reasonable access to collect the goods.

Corresponding legislation in Northern Ireland is the Unsolicited Goods and Services (Northern Ireland) Order 1976.

Weights and Measures Acts 1963 and 1979

Under these Acts, it is an offence if the quantity of the contents (weight, volume, or in a few cases, the number) is not marked on the container of most packaged grocery items and many other goods. Items such as meat, fish, cheese and sausages (frequently sold as pre-packs in self-service shops) must either have their weight marked on the package, or the weight must be made known before purchase. However, not all pre-packed goods must be marked; for example, everyone recognises a one-pint milk bottle. There are also exceptions in the case of small packets. The Acts also make it an offence to give short weight or inadequate quantity, and to mark goods with a wrong indication of their amount.

Most pre-packed goods (such as sugar, butter, tea, flour) must be sold in prescribed metric quantities – for example, flour can be sold only in quantities of 125, 250, 500 and 1,000g (or in multiples of 500g). A few foods must still be sold only in prescribed imperial quantities – for instance jam, where the 12oz and 1lb sizes are most popular. But the 1963 Act is being gradually amended to allow metric quantities. During the changeover period pre-packs in metric sizes must also show the imperial equivalent and be marked 'METRIC PACK'.

The 1979 Act introduced the 'average system' of quantity control for certain packaged goods. Under this system responsibility for the contents of these packages has largely switched from the retailer to the packer, who must make them up so that the quantity on the container is within certain tolerances laid down in the legislation. Enforcement generally takes place on the packing line, with direct control over some 180 million packages a year compared with the 5½ million packages that used to be checked at retail level under the 'minimum system'.

Packers, importers and traders who do not conform to the weights and measures laws can be prosecuted and fined.

Local authorities are responsible for enforcing the legislation and ensuring that weights, measures and scales are accurate. (In Northern Ireland, the Trading Standards Branch of the Department of Commerce is the enforcement authority.)

Things you should know when buying services

What is a 'service'?

'Services' include such things as car parks, holidays, TV hire, dating agencies – that is, contracts where no sale of goods is involved or those cases where the contract includes both a service and the supply of goods. Typical of the latter type of service, what lawyers call 'contracts for work and materials', are car and building repairs and double glazing.

Under common law, those who offer any kind of service must carry it out in a proper and workmanlike way, or to a standard you have agreed. Their obligations also extend to supplying goods that work properly and are correct for the job, when these form part of a contract for work and materials (for example, fitting a new clutch of the right sort to your car). They must also take care of any property you leave in their possession and make sure you are not injured or your property damaged as a result of their negligence. If they fail to do any of these things you can claim compensation from them.

Hired goods must be reasonably fit for their normal purpose, and traders cannot 'contract out' of this obligation.

Estimates and quotations

Before you ask a trader to tell you how much he will charge for a particular job, decide whether you will accept his good guess (what most people think of as an 'estimate') or whether you want a price which he must stick to (usually known as a 'quotation'). Whichever kind of price indication you settle for, make sure you get it in writing, properly itemised. He may charge for doing this, but even for a small job you may save money in the long run.

Because many repairs are hard to assess in advance (particularly for cars and buildings), few traders will commit themselves to quoting a fixed price. Instead, they prefer to quote a basic sum, and add a statement to the effect that this doesn't include anything else they might discover in the course of their work. When you accept an estimate like this, insist that the trader asks your permission to continue with the work as soon as it looks as though his estimate is going to be significantly exceeded (he is, however, entitled to pass on any increase in VAT).

It is always a good idea to ask for estimates from more than one trader. But don't automatically choose the trader who submits the lowest price. Try to settle on a trader whose work you have seen or who has been recommended by friends or neighbours. Quality is just as important as price.

For quotations relating to credit or hire agreements see page 35.

Completion dates

It is sometimes important to have a service job done by a certain date (for example, boots repaired in time for a walking holiday, or plumbing to be completed before the plasterer comes). If time is an essential term of the contract, agree it in writing before work starts. Then if the service firm lets you down you can cancel the contract and claim compensation.

Trade Descriptions Act 1968

The Act, as it refers to goods, is described on page 20. The same provisions apply to services, except that a trader commits an offence only if he knows the description of the service he is providing is wrong, or if he doesn't care whether it is true or not. Examples of the kind of advertised phrase which must be accurate are '24-hour dry cleaning', 'while-you-wait repairs', and 'the hotel is only a half-kilometre from the beach'.

Unfair Contract Terms Act 1977

Some firms try to escape their responsibility by using 'exclusion clauses' or 'disclaimers' on their premises, tickets, contracts or booking forms – for example, 'Articles left at owner's risk', 'We take no responsibility for. . .', 'Departure times subject to variation without notice'. These statements try to limit the firm's responsibility for any loss you may suffer or for any damage to you or your property because of their negligence or failure to carry out their side of the contract properly. But they are not valid unless the firm can prove, in court, that the terms are fair and reasonable in the circumstances. And the notices cannot limit the firm's responsibility if personal injury or death is caused through the firm's negligence.

Estate Agents Act 1979

The Director General of Fair Trading has two main powers. He can ban someone from engaging in estate agency work (that is, acting for clients in connection with buying or selling property) if he thinks that the agent is unfit to undertake such work. The ban can apply to all or certain aspects of the estate agency work, or relate to certain parts of the country. Alternatively, the Director General can warn the agent that if he continues to operate in certain undesirable ways he will be considered unfit and therefore banned.

An agent must give you certain information, including details of his charges, before you engage his services. He must declare any personal interest he may have in the transaction, be it buying or selling a property.

If you give an agent a contract or pre-contract deposit, he must pay it without delay into a special 'client' account and keep records which clearly show what he has done with any of your money in that account. In certain circumstances the agent may have to pay interest on your money while it is in his possession.

Pre-contract deposits are not permitted in Scotland.

What else you should know about dealing with traders

Deposits

You may see something in a shop which you'd like to reserve until you've got enough money to pay for it. So you put down a deposit. Or you order something not in stock (or to be made specially for you) and agree to pay part of the price in advance to show you intend to buy. Similarly, you may be asked for a deposit towards the materials and labour costs of a service to be done later, for example, re-roofing your house.

In all these cases you are making a binding contract with the trader, so that if later you change your mind about wanting the goods or service the trader could be entitled to keep your deposit. He could even sue you for up to the full amount of the goods or work, and, as in the case of a builder, for loss of profit on other work turned away.

Sometimes it is possible, and desirable, to negotiate a contract allowing you to cancel or alter arrangements in certain circumstances without financial loss (nobody would want the builder to plaster the walls of a home extension before the electrician had done the wiring). But make sure any special arrangement made with the trader is put in writing at the outset, otherwise it may be hard to prove later.

Statements of satisfaction

Sometimes you are asked to sign for goods delivered to your door. This is a reasonable request if proof of delivery is the motive for getting your signature. But occasionally the docket asks you to agree that the goods are satisfactory, and such a statement might prevent you from seeking your rights in the courts. In this situation it is best, on the whole, not to sign or, if you do, qualify your statement with 'I have not examined the goods' or some similar expression.

The same advice applies to a trader's request for a statement about satisfaction for a repair or service performed. It may be safe to sign for a hem shortened, provided you've tried on the garment and found it satisfactory. But it is not a good idea to commit yourself to saying the central heating has been installed correctly: it could play up the minute after you put pen to paper!

Guarantees

When you buy new goods you often get a manufacturer's guarantee (or warranty) with them. Some stores also offer guarantees on their goods – mainly electrical appliances – and so do some secondhand-car dealers.

People used to say you shouldn't sign manufacturers' guarantees as they often had expressions which implied you had no rights against the seller – for example, 'All conditions or warranties whether expressed or implied by statute or otherwise are excluded'. Since December 1978, however, it has been illegal to put any term like this into a guarantee and even if a manufacturer still includes such a statement, it doesn't mean anything and you can ignore it. So it is now usually worthwhile accepting the extra benefits a manufacturer's guarantee offers. It may offer to replace free of charge a major part of, say, a TV set for as long as five years. Or on some goods, notably sweets, it may offer to replace them if they are not up to standard, and to refund the postage.

Read the terms of a manufacturer's guarantee carefully. Along with the promises there may be conditions. You may be liable for any labour, postal or carriage charges involved in repairing/replacing faulty parts; or you may claim against the manufacturer only up to six months from date of purchase. If your guarantee contains terms like these, you would probably be better off claiming against the seller if the goods proved defective. In any case, under the Sale of Goods Act it is the **seller** who is responsible for the goods, even if you have signed a manufacturer's guarantee.

If you are entitled to reject faulty goods and want your money back, you should always claim against the seller: manufacturers usually undertake only to repair or replace goods, not to refund money.

29

Service companies, too, sometimes guarantee their work – for instance, 'Woodworm treatment – guaranteed effective for 20 years'. Such a guarantee may offer valuable extra benefits but don't place too much weight on it – the firm may have ceased trading long before the 20 years is up.

If you decide to accept a guarantee (usually by completing and returning a card within a certain period), keep it together with some proof of the purchase such as the receipt. You might find the latter useful if you wish to claim against the seller or, having forgotten to post the card, want the manufacturer's help.

Problem areas

Doorstep salesmen, sales representatives at 'parties' in private homes, or 'barkers' at one-day sales set up in such places as village halls and hotels – all are bound by the Sale of Goods Act (see page 5). The great majority of such traders are reputable and fair, and many firms who sell their goods in your home have agreed to follow a Code of Practice (see page 43). Unfortunately there are some who play on people's emotions and gullibility and a few, regrettably, are rogues. 'Caveat emptor' ('let the buyer beware') is a particularly apt phrase when buying goods or services from some of these traders! Here are some points to watch.

Buying from a doorstep salesman

- Check he is who he says he is (reputable companies give their salesmen identity cards).

- Don't feel obliged to buy anything if you don't really want to.

- Apart from minor purchases, it might be as well to find out what similar goods cost in the shops before agreeing to buy.

- Compare estimates from other firms for house repairs or improvements. (Some of the worst instances of cheating have been by 'fly-by-night' tradesmen offering to resurface a path or repair the roof.)

- Never pay in full before receiving the goods or service. If you pay a deposit, insist on a receipt with the firm's name and address on it.

- Don't sign **anything** without reading it carefully first.

- If you do buy, find out and keep the firm's name and address in case of problems later. (It isn't much use having rights against the seller if you can't find him!)

- Unless you're buying on hire purchase or credit sale, you have no right to change your mind about the purchase later.

31

- Make sure you know the true cost involved when buying on credit. Your right to cancel a credit agreement signed in your home is explained on page 40. See also **On the doorstep,** page 41.

Some businesses that sell from door to door are members of the Direct Selling Association, a trade body which has issued a Code of Practice for its members to follow. The address is on page 58.

Buying at 'parties'

Millions of pounds worth of goods (including plastic containers, cosmetics, jewellery and clothing) are sold each year at organised parties and coffee mornings in private homes.

- Don't feel obliged to buy things you don't really want, just to please the hostess or agent.

- Try to compare the goods being offered, and the prices charged, with similar goods in the shops.

- Find out if you can reject goods you've ordered in case you don't like them when they arrive.

- Be sure to note the name and address of the firm, **and the agent,** in case you need to complain or exchange the goods later.

- If you are the hostess, tell the guests what the party is for when you issue invitations.

Many businesses that sell goods at organised parties are members of the Direct Selling Association (see **Buying from a doorstep salesman**, page 30).

Buying at one-day sales

Some local authorities have drawn up codes of practice in co-operation with local chambers of commerce and organisations who may hire out premises for one-day sales. Such codes make the trader display his name and address on all advertising material and at the hall itself, and to conduct the sale according to certain fair trading practices. If you attend a one-day sale you would do well to remember the following points:

- Sometimes the low-priced goods featured in the advertisements are never offered for sale.

- At some sales all sorts of unfair promotional gimmicks are used like giving away 'free' goods or refunds to 'planted' buyers to encourage genuine customers to expect similar treatment.

- Be suspicious if the salesman won't let you examine the goods. (Some rogues **display** good quality articles but actually **sell** similar items of inferior quality – this is called 'switch selling'.)

- If you do buy something, insist on a receipt, giving full details of the trader's name and address.

Buying now, paying later

What is credit?

Taking out a mortgage on a house; raising a cash loan to pay for an unexpected repair to it; buying a TV set on hire purchase or clothes on a budget account; paying for a season ticket by credit card – all are ways of borrowing money or using credit. 'Buying now, paying later' is certainly convenient and something a great many people are doing today. It can make good financial sense, provided you're sure that paying out of savings wouldn't be cheaper in the long run and that you can afford to keep up the repayments.

Think carefully before buying anything on credit. Repayments almost always include a charge, normally called 'interest', for borrowing the money. Interest rates can be high, particularly in periods of inflation. Sometimes additional charges are included in an agreement, such as administration fees or maintenance charges, and the trader may calculate interest on these as well.

Interest rates can vary considerably. This is because some types of credit cost more to administer, or because the lender may charge more for a particular agreement if he feels it carries a high risk. Interest rates may also vary between firms offering the same kind of credit – for example, the banks, finance companies or insurance companies which compete for your custom. It therefore pays to shop around for the best credit terms available **to you.** For instance, if you regularly have a healthy current bank account it could be worth asking the manager for an overdraft or a personal loan, as these could be a cheaper way of buying certain goods than hire purchase or using a credit card.

Remember, too, that some credit agreements tie you to a particular maintenance contract for, say, a TV set. In such cases you might find it cheaper to look for alternative credit sources and make your own maintenance arrangements.

How to compare credit offers

Regulations under the Consumer Credit Act 1974 lay down rules about what credit information must be displayed on price cards, in window displays, and in all types of advertisement (including those on TV and radio). They also cover the way that the information must be displayed. The sort of information in advertisements you should look for is:

- the rate of charge for the credit, or, as it is often called, the **APR** – short for **Annual Percentage Rate.** This is the cost of borrowing the money, worked out as a yearly percentage.

- the basic price of the goods or service – that is, the cash price.

- the deposit.

- the period of the loan.

- the amount and frequency of payments, and what the whole credit deal will add up to.

- whether or not you will have to offer any security for the loan.

Because the APR must be worked out in a standard way and include all the charges you have to pay to obtain the credit, you can compare one type of credit with another and one trader's terms with another.

If there is any information you need which is not contained in an advertisement offering credit, ask for a written quotation. This must give the APR and all other relevant details. You can ask for written quotations from several traders and choose the best deal. And don't forget, when you are buying from retailers, you are not obliged to use the credit facilities they offer – you may be able to find a better credit deal elsewhere, for example, a personal loan.

No price card, window display, or other advertisement may claim to offer 'interest free' credit if all the repayments add up to more than the price you would have paid if you had paid cash. Neither can they claim to offer 'cheaper' or 'easier' credit than anyone else, unless they show figures to prove it.

Types of credit

Listed below are some of the more popular types of credit.

Bank overdraft   likely to be the cheapest loan available, provided you have a current account with the bank. You get permission to overdraw on your account up to an agreed amount and for a certain period. Repayment of the loan is made as you pay money into your account. Variable interest on the amount remaining 'in the red' is calculated on a day-to-day basis. The manager may charge a fee for a large overdraft and ask for security, such as the deeds of your house or an insurance policy. He can insist on repayment in full at any time.

Bank ordinary loan   available to bank customers only and usually for large amounts for a particular purpose approved by the manager – a loft extension to your house, for example. You agree with him the time you'll take to repay the loan and he may ask you to provide security (see **Bank overdraft**). Variable interest is charged and usually at a little higher rate than an overdraft.

Bank personal loan   available to anyone, though security may be requested from a non-customer. There is usually up to three years for repayments, but more for certain purposes such as home improvements. Interest is at a fixed rate.

Budget account   offered by many stores, allows you to spend up to a certain limit, for example, 15 times the £20 you decide you can afford to repay each month. You may spend up to £300, but must never owe more than this. As you pay back, so you can buy something else, provided you stay within your limit. Interest (often called a 'service charge' or 'surcharge') is charged on any amount outstanding at the end of a specified period (usually a month). Banks also operate budget accounts which are useful for spreading the repayments of your regular bills.

Credit card   issued by a bank or other finance company, allows you to pay for goods or services wherever it is accepted, including abroad. You are given a 'credit limit' which means you may have up to that amount outstanding at any one time. A monthly statement shows all the transactions you have made and the amount you owe, including any credit charge. Some companies insist on repayment of the whole sum outstanding, so you get only a few weeks' credit. (Instead of interest they charge you an annual membership fee.) With others you have to pay back a small minimum amount, or more if you wish. If you pay up in full each month, you will not be charged any interest. (Note that this concession doesn't apply to cash loans which can be obtained with this type of credit card.)

Many chain stores and supermarkets issue their own credit cards; some people hold several cards to cover their shopping needs.

The method of calculating interest varies greatly from card to card. You should therefore read the bank's or company's terms carefully.

Credit sale   similar in some ways to hire purchase except the goods belong to you at once – offered by shops for the purchase of goods. You normally have to pay a deposit, then equal weekly/monthly instalments over a fairly short period (usually up to nine months). Interest is at a fixed rate throughout the agreement, but varies slightly from shop to shop. A few stores offer interest-free credit for certain goods.

Finance company personal loan   used to pay for a specific and major item, and commonly arranged for you by department stores, car dealers and some electricity and gas boards. You might, however, get a slightly cheaper loan direct from another finance company, so shop around. The minimum you can borrow is around £100 or £200, and you may be asked for security (see **Bank overdraft,** page 36). The repayment is up to three years. These loans can be expensive.

Hire purchase (HP) probably the best-known way of buying on credit, and some people use the term to describe any sort of credit arrangement.

As with a **credit sale,** you buy goods by instalments (though the repayment period is usually much longer). But they do not belong to you until you've paid all the instalments – up to then you're simply hiring. However, there are laws which prevent the owner (usually a finance company) from reclaiming the goods without a court order. You, of course, mustn't sell the goods until they are legally yours.

Interest is at a fixed rate throughout the agreement. It varies from supplier to supplier but can be one of the more expensive ways to borrow.

A person who buys a car or motor cycle without knowing it is the subject of an outstanding HP agreement is normally protected. Finance companies have a register of motor vehicles being bought on HP – you can check through a Citizens Advice Bureau (see page 55) or motoring organisation.

Mail order credit offered by the large catalogue companies, who may use their agents to collect your repayments. The credit is often described as 'interest free', but this expression can be used only where all the repayments add up to the cash price.

If you send your repayments by post, make a careful note of these. Sometimes disputes can arise about alleged arrears.

Moneylenders' loans can be convenient, as they arrange many types of loan. Some will lend to almost anyone, often when no-one else will, and they will often call to collect repayments. For these reasons they charge very dearly for their services. Even though the charges are reduced when the loan is secured they can still be extremely high, sometimes more than the sum borrowed.

Mortgage lending offered mainly by building societies, banks, insurance companies and local authorities. Your property acts as the security. It is one of the cheapest ways of borrowing because of the high degree of security and consequent low risks taken on by the lender.

Credit unions formed by groups of people with a common bond. Members make regular savings to form a pool of money, from which they can borrow. Loans are usually quite small, but this depends on your savings record.

Trading checks and vouchers provided by specialist companies, can be exchanged for goods (mostly clothing and soft furnishing) in shops which accept them. An agent calls at your home and supplies a 'check' for any amount between £1 and £30. You repay him in weekly instalments usually over 20 weeks, including a charge for credit outstanding. ('Vouchers' are for larger amounts and repayable over much longer periods.)

Check trading is more common in some parts of the country than others. Although a convenient way of borrowing, it is normally quite expensive.

Signing agreements

Credit and hire agreements are legally binding so it is important to read them carefully and understand thoroughly the terms offered before signing. For example, check to see whether you're entitled to any rebate if you settle up early. **Never** sign a blank form!

With all **HP** agreements and **credit sale** agreements over £30, certain information must be given on the form – cash price, amount and date of each instalment, and total purchase price. If you sign an agreement at home either you must be given one copy of the agreement on the spot or, if the agreement was sent to you, a copy must be sent with it. Whether the first copy was handed to you or sent by post, a second copy must be sent within a week. This is your record of the HP or credit sale agreement. You then have a few days' cooling-off period in which to change your mind (details are on the form). But if you sign **any** kind of credit agreement in a shop or in a finance house, there is no cooling-off period.

Think carefully if you're asked to be a guarantor for somebody else's agreement. You are fully responsible for the debt if the buyer can't keep up the payments, so ask yourself 'Can I afford the amount involved?' Make sure you get copies of the documents.

Hire

When you hire (or rent) goods, you are not given the option to purchase them – but note the special case of **Hire purchase,** page 38. Hiring things that you're not likely to use often (or ever again), such as the heavier do-it-yourself tools, can make good financial sense. But think carefully before agreeing to hire anything for a long period. Ask yourself whether you can afford to keep up the payments, and whether it wouldn't be cheaper to buy the goods outright. Find out whether free maintenance or repair is included in the deal – for certain items, such as a TV set, this could be a 'plus' factor for hiring.

Keeping up the payments

If you get into difficulties with the payments or receive a notice of default, discuss your problem **as soon as possible** with the shop or finance company. Depending on the type of agreement you have with them, they may allow you a longer time to pay. (It is, of course, possible that they sent you a notice in error.) If you're in trouble, don't hesitate to go to your local consumer adviser for help (see page 54).

If you're hiring (or buying on HP) certain goods – such as a car or a TV set – find out whose responsibility it is if they are stolen or damaged. If it is **your** responsibility, think seriously about having them insured.

Even if not made compulsory by the lender, think also about taking out insurance against death, sickness or unemployment when you commit yourself to any substantial credit agreement – for example, double glazing or house purchase.

Consumer Credit Act 1974

Under this Act, nearly all businesses which offer credit or hire or which are involved with credit in some way (such as debt collectors, credit reference agencies) must be licensed by the Office of Fair Trading and their names kept on a public register. Only those fit to be in a business concerned with credit get licences. Licences can, of course, be taken away. If you feel you have been unfairly treated in a transaction involving credit tell your local Trading Standards Department (see page 54).

Apart from the rules governing advertisements and quotations for credit, which help you shop around for the best deal, the Act and its regulations cover other aspects of credit affecting consumers. Here are some of the more important.

On the doorstep
Traders must not call univited to your home, or stop you in the street, to offer loans or to put you in touch with those able to get you a loan. However, provided they are licensed to do so, they may call on you or stop you in the street to sell goods or services available on credit.

It is also illegal for traders to send you a credit card you haven't asked for, or to send anything through the post to people under 18 inviting them to borrow money or obtain other credit facilities.

Brokers' fees

If you have asked a broker to arrange a loan (including a mortgage), he mustn't charge more than £1 fee, commission or other charge, if you don't sign an agreement with the potential lender within six months. If you have paid more than £1 in these circumstances, the excess must be returned. However, if you were looking for a loan of more than £5,000, the broker can also charge you for things like survey fees.

Refused credit?

A trader doesn't have to give you credit or hire out goods, nor does he have to say why he won't do so. You have, however, the right to ask for the name and address of any credit reference agency he may have consulted about you and any inaccurate information held on you put right. Full details of this protection under the Act are given in the free leaflet **No credit?** (inside back cover).

Equal liability

Normally, if goods or services bought on credit prove faulty you are entitled to complain to the seller about them. But there's always the possibility that the seller has become bankrupt, gone into liquidation, or just refuses to co-operate, leaving you with an expensive item that doesn't work and that you're still paying for!

Under the Act, whoever provides the credit is **equally** liable with the seller, where the buyer has a claim against the seller, for any breach of contract or misrepresentation. (This applies to credit agreements entered into on or after 1 July 1977, where the cash price is more than £30 and less than £10,000.)

If you are buying on HP, the company providing the credit is in law the seller. So, strictly, you should complain to the HP company first. But, provided the supplier of the goods is still trading, it is best to contact him first.

Occasionally the supplier of the goods arranges his own finance, so supplier and seller are one and the same person.

Equal liability doesn't apply where you have been lent money to spend as you wish – that is, where the loan is not tied to the purchase of some specific item or service.

Extortionate credit

If you think you're being charged an extortionately high amount for any kind of credit agreement (whenever made), you can say so before a court. If the court agrees, it can help in various ways. For example, it can order the lender to repay unreasonable interest charges. But bear in mind that because certain kinds of credit cost more than others, your view of what is 'extortionate' may not be the court's! Before taking action, consult a consumer adviser (see page 54).

Codes of Practice

Under the Fair Trading Act 1973, the Director General of Fair Trading has a duty to encourage trade associations to draw up Codes of Practice – rules for their members to follow which should provide a better deal and improved standards of service for customers. To show he supports a Code of Practice, a trader usually displays his trade association's symbol on his premises. Symbols may also be displayed in advertisements, leaflets and brochures.

The advantage of Codes of Practice is that traders are expected to observe them in spirit as well as to the letter. Codes can therefore contain provisions which legislation couldn't practicably include (such as a promise to deal with complaints promptly and politely). They can be tailored to the particular circumstances of each trade or industry, and be adjusted as needs arise. By contrast, changing the law is time-consuming and expensive, and puts an extra burden on those who have to enforce it.

New Codes continue to be negotiated but the panel below shows the products and services covered by them at present. The kind of points they include are: better pre-shopping information; improved standards in the supply of goods or services; clear price displays; realistic estimates for delivery of goods or completion of repairs; prompt and helpful servicing arrangements; prohibitions on unfair or misleading trade practices; and staff training. All the Codes provide for a way of pursuing disputes which it has not been possible to sort out with the trader. Some of them also have an arbitration scheme – not to be confused with the simplified system for settling small claims in the County Courts of England and Wales and Northern Ireland, which is also referred to as arbitration (see page 49).

The names and addresses of the associations which have Codes of Practice and which deal with complaints are on pages 56-64 together with brief details of the Codes.

Leaflets giving fuller information on most of the Codes are listed facing page 68.

Did you know there are now Codes of Practice covering the following goods and services?

Buying at 'parties' in private homes
Buying by post (see **Mail order**)
Cars (new and used) and repairs/servicing
Doorstep selling
Double-glazing
Dry cleaning
Electrical goods and repairs/servicing
Footwear and repairs
Funerals
Furniture
Laundering
Mail order
Package holidays
Photography
Postal services
Telecommunications

Look out for labels

Here are some of the main labels you will see in shops, giving advice, information or warning. More are coming into use all the time.

British Electrotechnical Approvals Board

Safety requirements have been laid down for the majority of domestic electrical appliances and the mark of the **British Electrotechnical Approvals Board** is your assurance that the product is safe.

British Standards Institution

The Kitemark appears on a wide range of products complying with standards laid down by the **British Standards Institution** – from car safety belts to pressure cookers.

The Safety Mark appears only on goods which comply with British Standards for safety. Examples are certain types of gas appliances and light fittings.

Manufacturers wishing to use either mark must first submit their products to BSI for testing, and there are periodic tests of the goods and factory.

The BSI has a **Consumer Standards Advisory Committee** at 2 Park Street, London W1A 2BS.

Design Council

Products with this label have been chosen by the **Design Council** as being well-made, pleasant to look at and practical in use. There is a design index which can be seen at the Design Centres at 28 Haymarket, London SW1Y 4SU, and at 72 Vincent Street, Glasgow G2 5TN.

National Inspection Council for Electrical Installation Contracting

Your local Electricity Board shop has a list of reliable contractors in your area, who may display this label. These contractors are regularly inspected and approved by the **National Inspection Council for Electrical Installation Contracting,** an independent non-profit-making organisation set up to protect the interests of electricity consumers against faulty, unsafe, or otherwise defective workmanship.

British Gas

Appliances labelled with this symbol have passed **British Gas** standards for performance, reliability, and fitness for purpose.

Home Laundering Consultative Council

A garment care label of the **Home Laundering Consultative Council** tells you exactly how to care for the garment to which it is attached, giving specific water temperatures and so on. A guide to the washing processes appears on all detergent packs, and washing machine instructions use the HLCC washing temperatures and terms.

Furniture safety

Under the **Consumer Safety Act** (see page 17), display labels must be attached to new upholstered furniture which is not resistant to lighted cigarettes, matches or (as illustrated here) both. Permanent labels must also be attached, warning of the dangers.

How to complain if things go wrong

If you think you've got a reasonable complaint about something you've bought, take it up with the seller – even though you may dislike making a fuss! You are not asking for a favour to have something put right that is faulty or doesn't do what was claimed for it; and complaining can help achieve higher standards for everyone.

If you think you have a genuine complaint, whether about goods or services, follow this four-step procedure to get the matter put right.

Step 1

Stop using the item and take it back to the shop (if you can) as soon as possible. Take a receipt or proof of purchase if you have one. (Remember, a trader cannot refuse to consider your complaint simply because you don't have a receipt.) Make sure you see a senior person: in a chain store or supermarket ask for the manager or contact the managing director at head office.

If your problem is a tricky one it may be better to write to the firm's manager or managing director. To be on the safe side you should use recorded delivery. Keep copies of all letters. Do not enclose receipts or other proof of purchase – just quote reference numbers or send photocopies.

If you phone, make sure you know the name of the person you're dealing with – you may need it later on. Afterwards jot down the date and time and what was said.

However you make your complaint, always stick to the facts and keep cool, calm and courteous!

If your complaint is about the unfit condition of food or food sold in dirty or unhygienic restaurants, cafes, shops, canteens, markets, stalls, delivery vehicles or suchlike, report the matter **without delay** *to your local Environmental Health Officer (see page 54). If possible you should do this before you contact the seller.*

Step 2

If complaining to the trader gets you nowhere, go for some expert help and advice from a local consumer adviser at a Citizens Advice Bureau, Consumer Advice Centre, or Trading Standards or Consumer Protection Department. You can find their addresses in the telephone book, or by asking at the Council headquarters or library.

The consumer adviser will ask you for all the details and then may write or phone the trader to check the facts. Because someone else is taking an interest in the problem, the two sides are often more readily able to reach an agreement, and the matter could end satisfactorily there.

You can find out more about local consumer advisers and enforcement officers on page 54. Other sources of advice and help are on pages 64-67.

Step 3

If still not satisfied, and if the trader you're dealing with is covered by a Code of Practice (your consumer adviser may be able to tell you if this is so), either you or the consumer adviser can complain to the appropriate trade association (see pages 56-63). Most trade associations like your complaint to be in writing, or provide a special form to be used for it. The trade association's staff will then do all they can to try to settle the dispute.

Step 4

Sometimes – though not often – all this isn't enough. You can take the matter further by bringing a court case against the trader (see **Going to court,** below).

If your complaint is against a trader who follows a Code of Practice which includes an arbitration scheme, you can apply to have your case judged by an independent arbitrator (in Scotland, an 'arbiter'), whose final decision is binding on both you and the trader. However, if you choose this method, you cannot later take your case to court, so it is important to make the right decision. Your consumer adviser will help here.

Going to court

Unfortunately, problems aren't always solved on the trader's premises or by a consumer adviser. Sometimes it is necessary to sue the trader in court for compensation.

If you feel you have a case for the courts, always discuss it with a consumer adviser first (see page 54). There are various ways in which the adviser can help, for example, by filling in the details of your case on court application forms if you're the sort of person who is flustered by official documents.

If the claim you want to make is only a small one, it is tempting to forget all about it rather than go to the trouble and expense of suing. But in recent years procedures have been introduced in all parts of the United Kingdom so that consumers can more easily bring small claims in the courts.

If your claim is large or complex and you need a solicitor to represent you, the consumer adviser will help you find one and tell you about **Legal Aid**. This is a scheme, available to those on a low income, whereby the Government pays all or part of a solicitor's bill.

In England and Wales the County Courts deal with claims of up to £5,000 and you could conduct your own case without any legal knowledge or help from a solicitor. County Courts are accustomed to people bringing their own action and you are given every opportunity to explain your case in full. Even if there is a lawyer on the other side, the proceedings are quite easy for you to follow. If the sum you are claiming is not more than £500 your case will usually be settled by 'arbitration'; you won't normally have to pay anything for the other side's lawyer even if you lose, but you would have to pay for your own costs.

If the sum is higher and both parties agree, the Registrar can order arbitration if this seems to him the best way of dealing with the case.

Cases heard by arbitration are speedy, in private and very informal. Lawyers are often not present and nobody wears wigs and gowns. The decision of the arbitrator carries just as much weight as an award given in court in public, but you cannot normally appeal against it.

Application forms are available from the court office (the address is in the telephone directory under 'Courts'). You give brief details of the claim and there is a fee to pay, which depends on the size of your claim.

If you want to know more about going to law in England and Wales there are two booklets produced by the Lord Chancellor's Office which you can get free from County Courts or Citizens Advice Bureaux. They are **Small Claims in the County Court** and **Enforcing Money Judgments in the County Court.** Useful advice and information can also be obtained from court staff.

In Scotland there is no arbitration system of the kind described above. There is, however, a summary cause procedure which is a low-cost way of dealing with claims of up to £500 in the Sheriff Courts. The leaflet describing this is called **Guide to the summary cause in the Sheriff Court.** It is available from consumer advisers and Sheriff Courts. If you go to the Sheriff Court, the Sheriff Clerk or one of his staff will help you complete the form and tell you what fees must be paid.

In Northern Ireland the County Courts deal with claims of up to £5,000. Informal arbitration for claims up to £300 is available. Ask your local consumer adviser, Trading Standards Officer, or court office (address in telephone directory) for the leaflet **Small Claims Courts.**

Who cares?

If you want to make a complaint or need advice, among the important things to know is 'who does what'. Various government departments have a role to play in making the laws, local authorities (in the main) with enforcing them. A wide range of official and independent organisations give advice and help. Some are concerned with giving information to consumers and upholding trading standards. Among these are the trade associations with Codes of Practice, and the consumer councils and committees of the public services. Others act as pressure groups to get laws changed or grievances put right.

The following lists contain many helpful references. There are, of course, many others which cannot be included in a small booklet like this. For example, there are other codes of practice and conduct, and many trade and professional bodies which are prepared to help with advice and complaints about their members. But remember that their main responsibilities are often to the individual traders and firms who belong to them (and, obviously, they can't help with complaints about traders or firms who are not members of any association).

Consumer advisers (especially Citizens Advice Bureaux) may hold lists of organisations that can help, and at your local library there are various reference books you can consult.

Government departments

The Department of Trade is responsible for a wide range of laws that protect consumers, as well as for keeping a watch on business competitiveness. It takes the initiative over government policy for consumer credit, insurance, trade descriptions, and weights and measures, as well as administering consumer safety legislation. The Department provides a grant for Citizens Advice Bureaux' central services. The Secretary of State makes appointments to a number of bodies that serve as watchdogs in the consumer interest.

The Ministry of Agriculture, Fisheries and Food is responsible for the laws relating to the composition, labelling and advertising of food, and public health standards in the production and handling of milk, the handling of meat in slaughter-houses, and the import and export of meat and meat products. There are Consumers' Committees (Room 641, Great Westminster House, Horseferry Road, London SW1P 2AE) to which complaints about potatoes and milk can be sent (Scottish milk complaints should be sent to Chesser House, Gorgie Road, Edinburgh EH11 3AW).

The Department of Health and Social Security (and in Wales, the Welsh Office) is responsible, generally speaking, for the law on food hygiene and safety.

The Home Office is responsible for many aspects of public safety, for example, explosives security, control of firearms, dangerous drugs and fire prevention.

The Lord Chancellor's Office is responsible for the civil law, and for the administration of the civil courts.

The Scottish Home and Health Department in general looks after the Ministry of Agriculture and Department of Health functions listed above.

The Department of Commerce, Northern Ireland has general responsibility for consumer protection in Northern Ireland. Other Northern Ireland departments deal with the additional functions outlined above.

Main sources of advice and help

Most consumer legislation is enforced by the local authorities (except in Northern Ireland, where different arrangements apply).

Trading Standards – sometimes called Consumer Protection or Weights and Measures – Departments

These investigate complaints and enforce laws relating to false or misleading descriptions or prices, inaccurate weights and measures and some aspects of the safety of goods, and of consumer credit. Responsibility for enforcing the law on some food matters, such as composition and labelling, also lies with them. If uncertain where to complain about any aspect of food and drink, first ask the Trading Standards Department and it will refer you to the correct department if it cannot help.

For the address of local Trading Standards offices, look in the telephone book under the local authority's entry (in Northern Ireland under Department of Commerce Area Trading Standards offices, or contact your District Council).

As suggested on page 47, try to sort out your complaint with the trader first. Trading Standards Officers are busy people and in some areas will help only if the law they enforce has been broken. They may refer you elsewhere for pre-shopping advice, or if a trader has not complied with his civil law obligations to you – for example, under the Sale of Goods Act.

Some local authorities have **Consumer Advice Centres,** usually close to main shopping areas. The staff, who normally come under the Trading Standards Department, give a wide range of information and advice to shoppers and traders, and deal with problems and complaints. A few centres give pre-shopping advice as well. Mobile advice centres operate in a number of town and country areas. (In Northern Ireland, the Consumer Advice Centres are run by the District Councils at Belfast, Londonderry and Newry.)

Environmental Health Departments

These enforce the legislation that covers the health aspect of food – for example, mouldy or contaminated food and drink and dirty places where food is stored, prepared, and sold.

Their work also covers cleanliness in other establishments used by consumers, such as hairdressing and beauty salons. In Northern Ireland, Environmental Health Officers deal with all food complaints, including those concerning composition and labelling. In London boroughs, the division of responsibility between Environmental Health Departments and Trading Standards Departments varies.

For the address of local Environmental Health Officers, look in the telephone book under the local authority's entry (in Northern Ireland under the District Council's entry).

Citizens Advice Bureaux

There are about 900 of these independent organisations up and down the country. They provide free, confidential help and advice.

Bureaux cover a much wider range of problems than just shopping: health, housing, employment, marital and social problems – in fact most things to do with day-to-day living. Some bureaux offer free legal advice available by appointment only. Many will agree to act as 'go-between' in disputes between traders and consumers.

Opening times of bureaux vary across the country, so it is a good idea to check before calling. Bureaux are listed in the telephone book under Citizens Advice Bureaux.

Organisations with Codes of Practice

Listed below are some of the organisations – mainly trade associations – which have Codes of Practice. Those which have negotiated Codes in conjunction with the Office of Fair Trading are marked with a ★ The main aspects of each Code are briefly indicated and leaflets, giving more information on most of them, are listed facing page 68.

Advertising

Advertising Standards Authority
2–16 Torrington Place
London WC1E 7HN
Tel: 01–580 5555

The ASA is an independent body which administers two codes:

The **British Code of Advertising Practice** applies to most forms of advertising which appear in the media and in cinemas, but does not cover radio and television advertising. The object of the Code is to ensure that all advertisements are legal, decent, honest and truthful. The Code also includes detailed rules about advertisements dealing with such matters as slimming, medicinal and health products, alcohol, smoking, finance, mail order and testimonials. Complaints referred to ASA will be investigated and, if necessary, taken up with the advertiser concerned.

The **British Code of Sales Promotion Practice** includes rules relating to competitions, the use of children in promotions, and the quality, value and suitability of goods offered (for example as 'free gifts', prizes, or 'reduced-price offers'). The complaints system is the same as for advertising.

Independent Broadcasting Authority
70 Brompton Road
London SW3 1EY

The **IBA Code of Advertising Standards and Practice** covers all television and independent radio advertisements. It says they should not play on fear or superstition, nor be excessively noisy. Any price comparisons made must be accurate and not misleading.

The Code pays particular attention to medicinal and health products, alcohol and financial advertising, and to references to guarantees and testimonials. Special rules apply to child audiences and the use of children in advertisements.

Cars

★ Motor Agents' Association
73 Park Street
Bristol BS1 5PS

**Motor
Agents Association**

★ Society of Motor
Manufacturers and Traders
Forbes House, Halkin Street
London SW1X 7DS
Tel: 01–235 7000

★ Scottish Motor Trade Association
3 Palmerston Place
Edinburgh EH12 5AQ
Tel: 031–225 3643

The MAA, SMMT and SMTA support a joint **Code of Practice for the Motor Industry.** This covers many aspects of the sale of new and used cars, including warranties and the accuracy of mileage readings. It also covers the repair and servicing of cars done by their members. There is a conciliation and arbitration scheme.

★ Vehicle Builders and
Repairers Association
Belmont House, Finkle Lane
Gildersome, Leeds LS27 7TW
Tel: Morley 538333

The VBRA Code covers car body repairs done by its members. There is a conciliation and arbitration procedure.

Direct Selling

★ Direct Selling Association
44 Russell Square
London WC1P 4JP
Tel: 01–580 8433

DIRECT SELLING ASSOCIATION

'Direct selling' covers goods sold at organised parties in private homes, and goods sold at the door.

The DSA Code requires hostesses to make clear to guests the purpose of a party. Customers have two weeks in which to change their minds on goods ordered and get their deposits refunded. All sales leaflets must show the company's name and address.

For doorstep sales, the Code requires representatives to carry identification cards, to carry company literature on the products/services offered, and to accept 'no' courteously.

DSA offers informal conciliation on disputes.

Double glazing

★ Glass and Glazing Federation
6 Mount Row
London W1Y 6DY
Tel: 01–409 0545

The code covers all members' business with consumers, whether direct or through retail outlets, from the initial promotion to after sales service. Features include: five-day cooling-off periods; contracts to set out the procedure to be followed when work is not completed on time; members must comply with BSI standards; a conciliation and arbitration scheme.

Electrical goods

★ Association of Manufacturers
of Domestic Electrical Appliances
AMDEA House
593 Hitchin Road
Stopsley, Luton
Beds LU2 7UN

Most British manufacturers of domestic electrical appliances are members of AMDEA. The Code covers repairs or servicing done by them or their service agents. It sets out standards for speed and quality of service, guarantees on paid-for repairs, and how long members should stock spare parts. There are conciliation and arbitration schemes to settle disputes.

★ Electricity Council (on behalf of the Area Electricity Boards and Consultative Councils in England and Wales); and the

★ Scottish Electricity Boards (together with the Scottish Electricity Consultative Councils) operate Codes that are similar to AMDEA's and cover goods serviced or repaired through Electricity Board shops. See under **Public services' Consumer/Consultative Councils,** page 64, for how and where to complain.

★ Radio, Electrical and
Television Retailers' Association
RETRA House
57–61 Newington Causeway
London SE1 6BE
Tel: 01–403 1463

RETRA's Code lays down standards for the sale as well as the servicing of electrical and electronic goods. The Association runs a Customer Conciliation Panel.

Footwear

★ Footwear Distributors' Federation
69 Cannon Street
London EC4N 5AB
Tel: 01–248 4444

Most shoe retailers who belong to the Footwear Distributors' Federation, backed by several other associations, follow the **Code of Practice for Footwear.** The Code says member shops should give improved standards of service to customers and offer more advice and information about shoe materials used. If something does go wrong, the shop should deal with complaints promptly. Shoes can be independently tested at the Footwear Testing Centre, and the shop must abide by the Centre's decision. There is a small fee to the customer, refundable if the report is in the customer's favour.

★ National Association of Shoe
Repair Factories
Leather Trade House
9 St Thomas Street
London SE1 9SA
Tel: 01–407 1522

NASRF represents major shoe repair establishments, some heel bars, shops with repair facilities and some large shoe chain shops.

The **Code of Practice for Shoe Repairs** requires members to display price lists and provide repair tickets giving the cost of the repair and collection date. Members must also correct faulty repairs and handle complaints promptly.

★ St Crispin's Boot Trades Association
St Crispin's House
Station Road
Desborough, Nr Kettering
Northants NN14 2SA
Tel: Kettering 760374

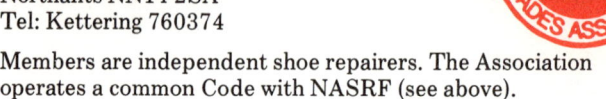

Members are independent shoe repairers. The Association operates a common Code with NASRF (see above).

Funerals

★ National Association of
Funeral Directors
57 Doughty Street
London WC1N 2NE
Tel: 01–242 9388

The Code requires members to provide a basic, simple funeral at an inclusive price; written estimates with detailed charges; and guidance on how to deal with death certificates etc. NAFD runs a conciliation service and independent arbitration to settle disputes.

NAFD does not include such independent services as florists and gravestone suppliers among its members.

Furniture

★ National Association of Retail
Furnishers
17–21 George Street
Croydon CR9 1TQ
Tel: 01–680 8444

★ Scottish House Furnishers'
Association
203 Pitt Street
Glasgow G2 4DB
Tel: 041–332 6381

The **Furniture Code of Practice** is supported by six associations (including manufacturers) but NARF and SHFA will each try to settle disputes about furniture bought in their members' shops.

Under the Code, furniture must have labels attached if information is not otherwise readily available, giving pre-shopping advice such as dimensions, construction details, care and cleaning instructions. The Code also requires retail members to quote realistic delivery dates and inform customers when these cannot be met.

Laundries and dry cleaning

★ Association of British
Launderers and Cleaners
Lancaster Gate House
319 Pinner Road, Harrow
Middlesex HA1 4HX
Tel: 01–836 7755

Most main laundries and dry cleaners are members of ABLC but not launderettes and coin-operated dry cleaners.

The Code covers all services normally provided including repairs and dyeing. Through its Customer Advisory Service, ABLC will deal with queries and complaints about member firms. If necessary, the Advisory Service can arrange test facilities at one of several fabric research establishments.

Mail order

★ The Mail Order Traders
Association of Great Britain
25 Castle Street
Liverpool L2 4TD
Tel: 051–227 4181

All the large catalogue companies are members. The MOTA Code provides for prompt delivery dates; the return of unwanted or faulty goods; servicing arrangements; and a complaints procedure.

★ Mail Order Publishers' Authority
1 New Burlington Street
London W1X 1FD
Tel: 01–437 0706

Members of the **Association of Mail Order Publishers** are firms which publish books, magazines or records sold by post.

Their Code covers the way goods are advertised and conditions about despatch. Members must review their debt collection methods and ensure that customers are not bothered without good reason. The Authority will try to settle unresolved disputes between you and one of its members.

Mail order protection schemes

Most newspapers, magazines and periodicals belong to associations which have mail order protection schemes. Under these schemes, senders are protected if they send off money for goods to an advertiser who goes into liquidation or bankruptcy before their goods are received. Provided they apply to the Advertisement Manager of the publication which carried the advertisement within the time specified, they should get their money back. (All publications which are members of an association supporting a scheme carry details about making a claim.) The Advertisement Manager may also investigate senders' complaints about late deliveries, refunds, faulty goods and the way goods are advertised.

The schemes do not cover classified advertisements or traders who advertise catalogues from which goods are then ordered.

British Code of Advertising Practice

The BCAP of the **Advertising Standards Authority** (see page 56) requires mail order traders to deliver goods (except plants and made-to-measure items) within 28 days, or to tell you if they cannot manage this. They must also promptly refund your money for unwanted goods returned undamaged within 7 days, or when goods are not delivered within 28 days and you consequently no longer want them.

All the mail order trade associations with Codes of Practice (listed above) require their members to abide by the BCAP.

Photography

★ Photographic Dealers' Association
84 Newman Street
London W1P 3LD
Tel: 01–323 4641

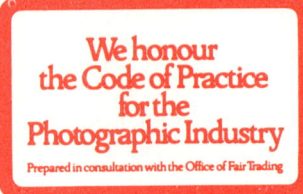

We honour the Code of Practice for the Photographic Industry

Prepared in consultation with the Office of Fair Trading

★ National Pharmaceutical Association
Mallinson House
40-42 St Peter's Street
St Albans, Herts AL1 3NT
Tel: St Albans 32161

★ Institute of Incorporated Photographers
Amwell End
Ware, Herts SG12 9HN
Tel: Ware 4011

★ Master Photographers Association
1 West Ruislip Station
Ickenham Road
Ruislip
Middlesex HA4 7DW
Tel: Ruislip 30876

The **Code of Practice for the Photographic Industry** is supported by ten associations, whose members must display the above symbol. The Code covers cameras, equipment, repairs, film developing and professional photography. Unresolved complaints are dealt with by the four associations above. If you are not sure which one to contact, write to the Photographic Dealers' Association, who will pass your letter to the correct organisation.

Postal services and telecommunications

★ There are two Codes of Practice, covering postal and telecommunications services. Copies of the Codes can be obtained at any post office.

Complaints about postal services should be made to the local Head Postmaster; and about telecommunications to the local Telephone Area Office (look on the back of your bill for the main contact points). If your dispute remains unresolved, contact:

Post Office Users' National Council
Waterloo Bridge House
Waterloo Road
London SE1 8UA

Travel

★ Association of British Travel Agents
55-57 Newman Street
London W1P 4AH
Tel: 01–637 2444

ABTA represents most well-known tour operators and travel agents.

The Code covers booking conditions, insurance cover, cancellations, alterations, surcharges, overbooking, and complaints about package holidays. ABTA operates a central fund to help safeguard customers' money if a member firm fails or defaults. It provides a conciliation service and has also arranged an independent arbitration scheme.

There are Tourist Boards for England, Scotland, Wales and Northern Ireland which are prepared to assist with complaints about a wide range of holiday services and facilities in the UK. Addresses can be obtained from local tourist information centres and local consumer advisers.

Public services' Consumer/ Consultative Councils

These include gas, electricity, postal and telecommunications services, British Rail or any other nationalised industry.

If you have a problem with the goods or services they provide, first try to sort it out with the people on the spot. If your problem is not about goods, look in the local telephone directory under 'Gas', 'Electricity', 'Post Office' etc. and find the precise department you need – 'Accounts', 'Sales', 'Servicing' or simply 'Customer Enquiries'. Or look on the back of your latest bill which usually has the main contact points. Explain your problem. If then you don't get satisfaction, contact the organisation's Consumer or Consultative Council – most have one.

Airlines

Air Transport Users' Committee
129 Kingsway
London WC2B 6NN
Tel: 01–242 3882

They can look into complaints against any airline, not just UK ones.

Airport facilities

Airport Consultative Committee – most major UK airports have one; at other UK airports complaints should be made to the airport manager.

Bus services

Contact the Local Traffic Commissioner. Address from local council offices. In London contact:
London Transport Passengers' Committee
26 Old Queen Street
London SW1H 9HP
Tel: 01–222 8777

British Rail

Transport Users' Consultative Committee.

Regional address from railway stations or telephone directory.

Coal and other solid fuels

Domestic Coal Consumers' Council
Gavrelle House
2 Bunhill Row
London EC1Y 8LL

The industry operates the Approved Coal Merchants' Scheme.

Electricity

Electricity Consultative Council for your area (address from bill, showroom or telephone directory). In Northern Ireland, the Electricity Consumers' Council.

Gas

Regional Gas Consumers' Council for your area (address from bill, showroom or telephone directory).

Postal services, telecommunications

See page 63.

Some other bodies to whom complaints can be made

Hearing aids

Hearing Aid Council
40a Ludgate Hill
London EC4M 7DE
Tel: 01–638 9226

No one, outside the NHS, may supply hearing aids unless registered to do so. The Council cannot obtain recompense on behalf of members of the public but can take disciplinary action against the supplier.

Insurance

'Doorstep' life assurance

Life assurance policies on which premiums are collected by agents who call at policyholders' homes at intervals of less than two months come within the official jurisdiction of the Industrial Assurance Commissioner:

Industrial Assurance Commissioner
17 North Audley Street
London W1Y 2AP
Tel: 01–629 7001

The Commissioner for Northern Ireland has his office at
43-47 Chichester Street, Belfast
Tel: Belfast 34121.

The trade association for this type of assurance is:

Industrial Life Offices Association
Aldermary House
10-15 Queen Street
London EC4N 1TL
Tel: 01–248 4477

Insurance brokers

British Insurance Brokers' Association
130 Fenchurch Street
London EC3M 5DJ
Tel: 01–623 9043

Complaints and enquiries relating to the part played by a broker, as opposed to an insurance company, may be referred to this association.

Life assurance

Life Offices' Association and
Associated Scottish Life Offices
Aldermary House
Queen Street
London EC4N 1TP
Tel: 01–236 1101

Complaints and enquiries relating to life assurance policies may be referred to the Life Offices' Association if the company concerned is a member.

Lloyd's

Advisory Division
Lime Street
London EC3M 7HA
Tel: 01–623 7100

This will deal with complaints about Lloyd's insurance if you
cannot obtain satisfaction from the broker concerned.

Non-life insurance

British Insurance Association
Aldermary House
Queen Street
London EC4P 4JD
Tel: 01–248 4477

This is the association to approach about complaints concerning
non-life (for example, motor, household, holiday) insurance if the
policy has been issued by one of its members. It has information
officers in most large towns.

Insurance Ombudsman Bureau

31 Southampton Row
London WC1B 5HJ
Tel: 01–242 8613

Personal Insurance Arbitration Service

The Chartered Institute of Arbitrators
International Arbitration Centre
75 Cannon Street
London EC4N 5BH
Tel: 01–236 8761

These schemes, between them, provide for the settlement of
disputes with a number of insurance companies.

Consumer bodies

Consumers' Association

14 Buckingham Street
London WC2N 6DS
Tel: 01–839 1222

National Consumer Council

The Council was established by the Government in 1975. It watches over consumers' interests and speaks up for the consumer to Government, nationalised industries, commerce, and public and private services. It has no statutory powers but carries out a wide range of research and publishes its recommendations. The Council does not deal with individual complaints. There are Councils for Northern Ireland, Scotland and Wales, and all four work closely together.

National Federation of Consumer Groups

Mrs. D. Freeman
Flat 1, 31 Sussex Square
Brighton BN2 5AB
Tel: 0273 602816

The Federation is the central organisation for voluntary local consumer groups. It can put you in touch with your local group or help you to start one. Or you can join the Federation as an individual member. Groups survey local goods and services, publish their reports, and campaign for improvements where necessary. (S.a.e. please.)

The Association tests, compares and reports on goods and services for some 650,000 subscribers to its five magazines – the best known being *Which?* Information on more general topics and problems which affect family and personal life is available in a series of paperbacks – details from Freepost, Hertford SG13 8BR (no stamp required). *Which?* gets no money from advertisements, industry or any other source which might endanger its independence. The Association also provides a consultancy service to local authorities setting up advice centres, together with training and information services.